Prayer Journal

1 Month Guide to Prayer, Reflection, Gratitude and Praise

Kristina Ducklow

© **Copyright 2018 by Joy Publishing & Marketing Corporation - All rights reserved**

This document is geared towards providing helpful and reliable information in regards to the topic and issue covered. The publication is sold with the idea that the publisher is not required to render accounting, officially permitted, or otherwise, qualified services. If advice is necessary, legal or professional, a practiced individual in the profession should be ordered.

- From a Declaration of Principles which was accepted and approved equally by a Committee of the American Bar Association and a Committee of Publishers and Associations.

In no way is it legal to reproduce, duplicate, or transmit any part of this document in either electronic means or in printed format. Recording of this publication is strictly prohibited and any storage of this document is not allowed unless with written permission from the publisher. All rights reserved.

The information provided herein is stated to be truthful and consistent, in that any liability, in terms of inattention or otherwise, by any usage or abuse of any policies, processes, or directions contained within is the solitary and utter responsibility of the recipient reader. Under no circumstances will any legal responsibility or blame be held against the publisher for any reparation, damages, or monetary loss due to the information herein, either directly or indirectly.

Respective authors own all copyrights not held by the publisher.

The information herein is offered for informational purposes solely, and is universal as so. The presentation of the information is without contract or any type of guarantee assurance.

The trademarks that are used are without any consent, and the publication of the trademark is without permission or backing by the trademark owner. All trademarks and brands within this book are for clarifying purposes only and are the owned by the owners themselves, not affiliated with this document.

To my dearest Ella,

You are my answered prayer.

I love you. Jesus loves you more.

If you stumble, make it part of the dance.

Cling to Him and never stop trusting Him.

Shine brightly for His glory!

This book wants to make you happy.

Are you ready to smile?

Introduction

"Prayer means talking over with Jesus everything that happens
from morning until night."- Basilea Schlink

Welcome! This prayer journal was a response to prayer and I'm so grateful you have found it in your hands. Whether you are a stranger to prayer or a prayer warrior, my intent was to design a tool that would draw you into a deeper relationship with Jesus.

To be honest, I don't "feel" like an authority on the topic of prayer. Consequently, I'm not going to teach you what it is and why it's important. I don't feel adequate for that level of education and I don't believe that's the purpose of creating this journal. My heart is to be real and honest about my journey and support you in your own. I pray that my vulnerability will give you the freedom to relax in prayer and not make it a religious burden that condemns you whenever you miss the mark.

For me, prayer is talking to Jesus about anything and everything. Prayer allows me to be intimate with Him, express my needs or concerns, and receive encouragement and guidance. If you are in a relationship with anyone, you already understand prayer. In the same way we talk to maintain closeness with others, we pray to stay in connection with Jesus. Honestly, more often than not, my time is usually spent talking and then struggling to sit still long enough to listen. Perhaps you can relate?

Not only does prayer necessitate a trust and dependence on Christ, it requires for me to humble myself and surrender to His authority. On the one hand, I am left in a position of vulnerability as I make my requests known to God. And on the other, I put my hope in a great belief that He will actually hear and be swayed by my requests.

Prayer can occur anytime, anyplace, as much or as little as needed, with spoken words, thoughts, or even groanings in your spirit. There are no formalities, postures or rules. What a wonderful privilege we have to freely commune with the God of all the universe! How truly remarkable that He gives us the ability to influence Him and make our desires known. We are blessed to be partakers in His plans and witnesses to His power.

My Story

I became a Christian at 19 years old and I recently celebrated my 15th year! I'm so grateful for this wild journey and I'm falling more in love with Jesus as I continue to receive new revelations of what He's done for me. Although I've been a Christian for a while, I haven't fully understood prayer and I'm still trying to make sense of it. I've heard testimonies of answered prayers and Christians raving about God's amazing power, but I haven't always been convinced. I figured: I'm a Christian, Christians pray, so I must pray too.

I feel embarrassed to be creating a prayer journal when that's been my experience. Nevertheless, I have come to see the power of prayer in my own life and have marveled at the ways God has answered my own private prayers. In 2014, within 6 months, I had a miscarriage, a friend pass away and my dog put down. While the dog dying was expected (she was old), the other 2 events were not. I was incredibly angry about my miscarriage because I wanted another child so badly. And the friend dying knocked me off my feet and put me on a sick leave from work as I struggled to cope. Through prayer, God reveled to me that He was sparing me from something that I could not yet see.

In hindsight, I see my miscarriage as a blessing in disguise and a catalyst for change. It catapulted me onto an amazing journey of health that I am presently enjoying today. The intensity of the situation pushed me to go beyond myself and see God working my pain for good (Romans 8:28). I truly believe others will be healed from my wounds and God will repay me double for my trouble (Zechariah 9:12, Job 42:10). My faith in God's promises makes the pain worth it for me.

"Praise be to the God and Father of our Lord Jesus Christ, the Father of compassion and the God of all comfort, who comforts us in all our troubles, so that we can comfort those in any trouble with the comfort we ourselves receive from God." 2 Corinthians 1:3-4

I don't always understand why He doesn't answer ALL my prayers or in the way I would like Him to, but I do know He answers. He sees the end from the beginning (Isaiah 46:10) and stands outside of time. His thoughts are higher than my thoughts and His ways are far beyond anything I can imagine (Isaiah 55:9). Therefore, I trust that He is using all for His glory and it will make sense when I'm in Heaven. Sometimes, it's in His kindness that my prayers have not been answered. Even though I don't know the future, I know the One who does.

"God answers all prayers, but sometimes His answer is 'no.'" – Dan Brown

As I look back on my journals from my single years, I marvel at the kind of prayers I prayed. Even though they were a far cry from my current prayers, I've realized that it isn't fair to compare. My life is different now: I have a husband, 2 young children and wrestled through 10 years of depression. My time is no longer my own and I've had seasons of great darkness. Through the years I have had to reinvent my connection with Jesus and find new ways to feel close and intimate with Him.

When I was single and had an undivided focus on Jesus, it was amusing to notice how I didn't feel good enough in my prayer life. Fast forward till now, I still feel like I'm not doing enough and I should always be doing more. Perhaps the lesson here is that my good enough IS good enough regardless of how I feel. My right standing with God is about what Jesus has done for me (Romans 3:22-26), not whether I "feel right" or by trying to do enough good works to please Him.

Therefore, my hope is for you to not feel the guilt and burden of daily trying to keep up. I've had previous journals where I'd set the intention to complete them EVERY day but then life happened. The result: I started to beat myself up, which initiated a vicious cycle of defeat. The cycle never ended well and I was often pushed further away from my goals.

Instead, I want to practice kindness, compassion and gentleness. If there are gaps in your journaling, that's understandable. Treat it as good data...teaching you what to do differently next time. If you were to get a flat tire, you wouldn't get out of the car and slash the other 3 tires. No! You'd fix the flat and then keep driving. I believe this concept holds true for your journaling as well. If you miss a few days, be kind. Pick up where you left off and keep going!

Several months ago I was reacquainted with the movie, "The War Room," while I was in the thick of great turmoil. Even though I didn't set up a prayer closet or commit to praying as much as I "should" have, the nature of my prayers changed. It was prayer that brought me through in the end - giving me peace, perspective and grace. The quiet confidence and joy I experienced, despite my circumstances, was profound and didn't make logical sense. But God promised to keep in perfect peace all those who trust in Him and whose thoughts are fixed on Him (Isaiah 26:3). I was able to offer compassion, let go of the outcome and trust that God was working all for my good.

Did you to catch my "should?" We have these ideas of how we think things "should" be, which results in feelings of guilt and condemnation. When things don't go the way we want or get worse, we wonder if it's our fault. Perhaps God is punishing us or we didn't pray enough? But no, no, no that's not true! God is full of grace, mercy and kindness. It's never about us, what we can do or how eloquent our prayers are. The foundation of our faith is that Christ did for us what we couldn't do for ourselves (Romans 8:3). It's all about Him! He gives us the power to please Him (2 Peter 1:3). He is the author and finisher of our faith (Hebrews 12:2). He sets us up to have a relationship with Him and provides all we need to be successful. Regardless of whether we do more or less, God still loves us the same! He IS love, therefore, He can't help but love. So take heart and keep praying. Cling to Jesus and never stop trusting Him!

How to Use This Journal

Each section of the journal was prayerfully and thoughtfully designed in order to produce two outcomes: to move you into a deeper relationship with Jesus and to stimulate gratitude and happiness. Complete as much or as little as you'd like for as many or as few days as you are able. Try to enjoy the process rather than feel stress, burden and obligation. Although you are not a failure if you don't follow through every day, you will greatly benefit from consistency. Your life is the sum of your choices and where you find yourself in ten years will be a reflection of the decisions you make today.

"Let it be your business every day, in the secrecy of the inner chamber, to meet the holy God. You will be repaid for the trouble it may cost you." Andrew Murray

Left Page - PRAY

The first page of each day is divided into 5 sections inspired by the acronym PRAY. The goal is to guide you through a process and provide some structure. Since we can often get overwhelmed with where to start, the PRAY framework will at least get you going.

"Our prayers lay the track down which God's power can come. Like a mighty locomotive, his power is irresistible, but it cannot reach us without rails." - Watchman Nee

Bible Verse: Pick a verse, any verse and write it in this box. You can even randomly open your Bible and see where your finger lands. Let this verse be the focus for your day. Take some time to ponder the verse, consider its context and think of how you can apply it to your life.

Praise "Father, I thank you for..."
Begin your prayer by praising and thanking God for who He is. You can thank Him for aspects of His character, what He did for you on the cross, or a previously answered prayer. We want to seek God's face, not His hand. Starting your prayer with praise will bring you into a place of humility and remind you of how great, awesome and powerful God truly is. The result will be increased faith needed to pray bold prayers.

Repent "I am sorry for..."

Next we recognize that we are nothing without God and we need Him to forgive our sins. Sin creates static in the communication lines with God and it's essential to clear up the noise by saying "sorry." We are unable to fill ourselves with God if we are full of ourselves. Therefore, when we surrender to God, He is able to pour life into our empty vessel. Search your heart and say you're sorry for whatever comes to mind. Then receive His forgiveness and be amazed by His mercy! He is more than happy to forgive and remove our sins (1 John 1:9): that was the point of His amazing work on the cross.

Ask "I pray for..."

Now that you've put God in His rightful place as Lord and Saviour, and you've positioned yourself in a place of humility, you are ready to start making your requests known. A daily prayer suggestion has been provided to help you get started. Pray for everything and anything...whatever is on your heart. There are no limits! The only condition is asking and believing! God is able to accomplish infinitely more than we might ask or think (Ephesians 3:20), and He promises that if we ask for anything in His name that He will do it for us (John 14:14).

"Look at a stone cutter hammering away at his rock, perhaps a hundred times without as much as a crack showing in it. Yet at the hundred-and-first blow it will split in two, and I know it was not the last blow that did it, but all that had gone before." - Jacob Riis

Yes/Yield "Lord, help me..."

The last step is to say "Yes" and "Yield" to His will. Tell God how you need faith to follow Him. You may need help understanding Scripture, or needing a revelation of His love, or requesting assistance with being obedient in a specific area of your life. Jesus came to heal the sick (Luke 5:31), so admit what you need help with.

Right Page - Questions and Prompts

The right page is divided into a morning and evening section. Do whatever works for you. There are no rules here.

Morning:

Gratitude "I am grateful for..."

Studies have shown that people who practice gratitude are happier. The Bible also instructs us to have a thankful heart. Use this space to express gratitude for the big or small. It can be as simple as giving thanks for the sun or the ability to breathe. You can give thanks for people, places, things, experiences, memories...whatever elicits a flutter of thankfulness in your heart. We can always find something to be grateful for even if there doesn't seem to be anything at all. Bare minimum: you can always thank Jesus for what He did on the cross because that was truly marvelous!

Abide "Jesus, I hear you say..."

Take the time to still yourself and listen for the Holy Spirit. God often speaks in a small quiet voice. Unfortunately, we can often be too busy talking and not actually listening. Do your best to tune your ear and linger long enough to hear what God is whispering in your heart. I'll be honest, this is the hardest part for me. I have a difficult time sitting still because suddenly everything else seems more interesting to me...like sweeping the floor. However, this is a skill of mindfulness and it needs to be practiced. The more you exercise this muscle, the longer you'll be able to train your focus. A million thoughts will enter your mind, which is totally normal. Acknowledge your thoughts and then redirect your attention. People often find grounding themselves in their breath helps to stay centered.

Declare "In Christ, I am..."

Finish your prayer time with affirming who you are in Christ. Renew your mind with what God says is true about you. Actually believe that you are fearfully and wonderfully made (Psalm 139:14), more than a conqueror in Christ (Romans 8:37), able to do all things in Him and through Him (Philippians 4:13). In and of ourselves we are nothing, BUT in Christ, we are everything! Although we had nothing to offer Him, He offered all He had to us. It's time to start proclaiming the truth instead of believing what others, the world, or we say is true about us.

Evening:

The purpose of these questions is to stimulate your joy as you train your brain to notice the positives, recognize God's blessings, and catch the ways you considered others. What you focus on you feel. Therefore, if you pay attention to how you are blessed and how you've been a blessing, you will increase your happiness and wellbeing. Success begets more success. Soon you'll be on a rampage to find more ways to serve.

You may wonder why I'm focusing on happiness because it doesn't seem to fit with the theme of prayer. My motive behind this book was to draw you into a deeper relationship with Jesus as a by-product of spending private time with Him. When we experience the presence of God, we are filled up, which results in us wanting to pour into the lives of others. The Bible says that Jesus came to give us life in abundance (John 10:10). He wants us to thrive in our lives so we can bring glory to Him and heal the world through His love. The choice is ultimately ours to be happy or not.

I recognize that choosing to be happy can be incredibly difficult when we are in a hard circumstance. It has taken me a ridiculously long time to finally grasp that I am able to choose my thoughts and attitudes. It's taken me even longer to realize that I, not events, or people or possessions, have the power to make me happy or unhappy. In the end, I choose which outcome I want. Even God affirms we have a choice between life and death. He urges us to choose life because then it will go well for us (Deuteronomy 30:19). He sets us up for success by giving away the answer: choose life!

Proverbs 17:22 tells us that a happy heart is good medicine. After several years of depression, I have finally come to believe that I am allowed to be happy and that my happiness actually serves God. When we are happy, it gives other people permission to be happy – it's good medicine! Happiness lifts their soul and they in turn give to others, which builds momentum. We can conquer evil by doing good (Romans 12:21) but we need to start allowing the force of good to manifest first with us.

"When you choose joy you feel good, and when you feel good, you do good. And when you do good it reminds others of what joy feels like and it might just inspire them to do the same." – Annoymous

Question 1:

"What made me smile today?"

"What am I excited about in my life?"

"What am I celebrating in my life?"

"What success did I have today?"

"What am I happy about in my life?"

"What am I proud of in my life?"

"What am I enjoying the most in my life?"

The first evening question rotates each day. I want to specifically clarify the word "celebrate" in the question, "What are you celebrating in your life?" Record something you've accomplished that you are excited about. I'm not talking about celebration in the context of a birthday. For example, you may be celebrating drinking a glass of water, or taking the stairs instead of the elevator, or saying "no" to a piece of chocolate cake. Keep it simple and let the excitement of your celebration gain traction as you celebrate more actions throughout the day. I personally like to give myself high fives or pats on the back when I catch myself. It's so energizing when we live out of a place of celebration rather than criticism. It makes us want to do more.

Question 2: "How did I see the hand of God?"

The second question encourages you to find the ways God has blessed you throughout the day. He's blessing us all the time but we don't always train our eyes to see it. Start paying attention and you will marvel at all the ways He is trying to love you.

Question 3: "In what ways was I a giver?"

The last question is asking you to notice the ways you have been a blessing to another. It's pretty obvious that when we give we feel happier. I've had to get over myself and trust that as I step out, my needs will be met. I've had reservations in the past about serving people because I was so consumed with depression and fear. I would often think, "What about me?" I finally began to understand that the joy I was longing for would increase if I made small steps to serve others. You'll never know till you get to the other side and find out that serving is actually awesome and God was right all along. Your acts of kindness don't need to be large. They can be as simple as a smile, opening the door for someone, or offering an encouraging word. The Bible tells us to "encourage each other and build each other up" (1 Thessalonians 5:11). I challenge you to encourage three people a day for a month and see how you feel. When we get our minds off ourselves, we start looking for ways to bless others. The more you are full of the love of God, the more you will naturally want to spread His love to others.

"Give, and it will be given to you. A good measure, pressed down, shaken together and running over, will be poured into your lap. For with the measure you use, it will be measured to you." Luke 6:38

Weekly Reflection

Take the opportunity to write down your weekly prayer requests and answered prayers. You can continually update these lists as the weeks go on. Naturally, your faith will grow as you notice the hand of God moving in your life. Seeing answered prayers gives us the reassurance that God hears us and the boldness to pray bigger prayers. They also provide us comfort during times when we need a reminder of God's faithfulness.

Highs: "What amazing things happened? How have these added to the quality of my life?"
Think about your past week and record your highlights. Use your amazing memories to build momentum for the future and to further engrave your memories into your brain. As a result, you will feel more energized with joy as you stack all these memories from week to week. Make sure to also give God thanks for His blessings.

Lows: "What did I learn? What can I do differently?"
Take an honest look at the week and consider what didn't go well. This isn't a place for judgment or shame. The point is to use this information as good data and then do something different. Insanity is when we do the same thing over and over while expecting different results. Don't drive yourself insane by going around the same mountain. Face yourself and do yourself a favor by making the necessary changes to create a better future. If you don't like something, you are the only one who can make the change, so take action! Remember to ask God for His power and grace. We can do nothing without Him (John 15:5).

Goal: "What's one step I will take to move closer to my purpose?"

Take the time to write down one practical, small action you can do this week in order to move forward in God's purpose for your life. You may have a specific God given vision that will never come to fruition if you don't take steps to make it happen. Therefore, write down your dreams so they can become a reality. Then do it!

Love Challenge: "What's one act of service or random kindness I will do?"

Lastly, I challenge you to step out and love! Have fun devising ways to serve: feed people who live on the streets, make a card for an elderly person, pay for someone's meal in the drive thru, or offer babysitting for a mother with young children. You don't have to do the challenge but it will be awesome for your soul if you do. Besides, God instructs us to love others as we love ourselves (John 13:34-35). Therefore, step out and try! You'll be so thankful you did when you see the gratitude and joy in others.

Notes:

In an effort to not be too structured, each week has several pages devoted to nothing at all or whatever extra space is need for. Use this area for sermon notes, extra prayers, or to record whatever you are studying or learning.

Bible Verse Coloring Page:

Unleash your creativity with these hand drawn weekly coloring pages. As you release your inner child, allow your mind to ponder and meditate on the Bible verses so they will take root in your soul and be written upon your heart.

Conclusion

My hope is for you to enjoy your prayer journey as much, if not more, than I have enjoyed the process of creating this journal for you. I pray that your heart will be enlightened with the wonders of God and you will know how long, high, deep and wide His love really is (Ephesians 3:18). May your love for Jesus shine brightly for all to see (Matthew 5:16) and "may the God of hope fill you with all joy and peace as you trust in Him" (Romans 15:13). Fix your eyes on Jesus and keep running the race He has set before you (Hebrews 12:1-2)!

Bible Verses on Prayer

If my people, who are called by my name, will humble themselves and pray and seek my face and turn from their wicked ways, then I will hear from heaven, and I will forgive their sin and will heal their land. 2 Chronicles 7:14

And pray in the Spirit on all occasions with all kinds of prayers and requests. With this in mind, be alert and always keep on praying for all the Lord's people. Ephesians 6:18

Then you will call on me and come and pray to me, and I will listen to you. Jeremiah 29:12

But I tell you, love your enemies and pray for those who persecute you. Matthew 5:44

And when you pray, do not keep on babbling like pagans, for they think they will be heard because of their many words. Matthew 6:7

Watch and pray so that you will not fall into temptation. The spirit is willing, but the flesh is weak. Matthew 26:41

The LORD detests the sacrifice of the wicked, but the prayer of the upright pleases him. Proverbs 15:8

I call on you, my God, for you will answer me; turn your ear to me and hear my prayer. Psalm 17:6

Be joyful in hope, patient in affliction, faithful in prayer. Romans 12:12

Answer me when I call to you, my righteous God. Give me relief from my distress; have mercy on me and hear my prayer. Psalm 4:1

The LORD is near to all who call on him, to all who call on him in truth. Psalm 145:18

Devote yourselves to prayer, being watchful and thankful. Colossians 4:2

The eyes of the LORD are on the righteous and his ears are attentive to their cry. Psalm 34:15

Pray continually. 1 Thessalonians 5:17

Therefore confess your sins to each other and pray for each other so that you may be healed. The prayer of a righteous person is powerful and effective. James 5:16

In the same way, the Spirit helps us in our weakness. We do not know what we ought to pray for, but the Spirit himself intercedes for us through wordless groans. Romans 8:26

One day Jesus told his disciples a story to show that they should always pray and never give up. Luke 18:1

Keep on asking, and you will receive what you ask for. Keep on seeking, and you will find. Keep on knocking, and the door will be opened to you. You parents—if your children ask for a loaf of bread, do you give them a stone instead? Or if they ask for a fish, do you give them a snake? Of course not! So if you sinful people know how to give good gifts to your children, how much more will your heavenly Father give good gifts to those who ask him? Matthew 7:7-11

But when you pray, go away by yourself, shut the door behind you, and pray to your Father in private. Then your Father, who sees everything, will reward you. Matthew 6:6

Don't be like them, for your Father knows exactly what you need even before you ask him! Matthew 6:8

He said to them, "When you pray, say: 'Father, hallowed be your name, your kingdom come. Give us each day our daily bread. Forgive us our sins, for we also forgive everyone who sins against us. And lead us not into temptation.'" Luke 11:2-4

You don't have what you want because you don't ask God for it. James 4:2

I tell you the truth, if you had faith even as small as a mustard seed, you could say to this mountain, 'Move from here to there,' and it would move. Nothing would be impossible. Matthew 17:20

One of those days Jesus went out to a mountainside to pray, and spent the night praying to God. Luke 6:12

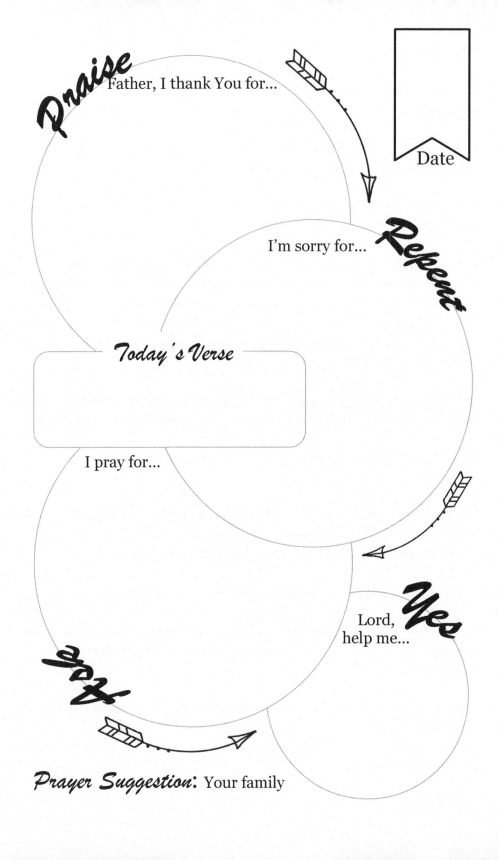

Gratitude

I am grateful for...

Abide

Jesus, I hear You say...

Declare

In Christ, I am...

What made me smile today?

How did I see the hand of God?

In what ways was I a giver?

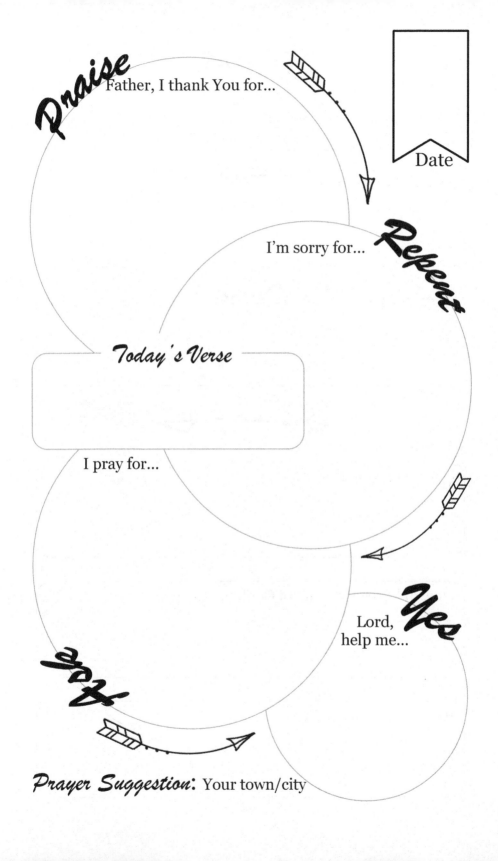

Gratitude
I am grateful for...

Abide
Jesus, I hear You say...

Declare
In Christ, I am...

What am I excited about in my life?

How did I see the hand of God?

In what ways was I a giver?

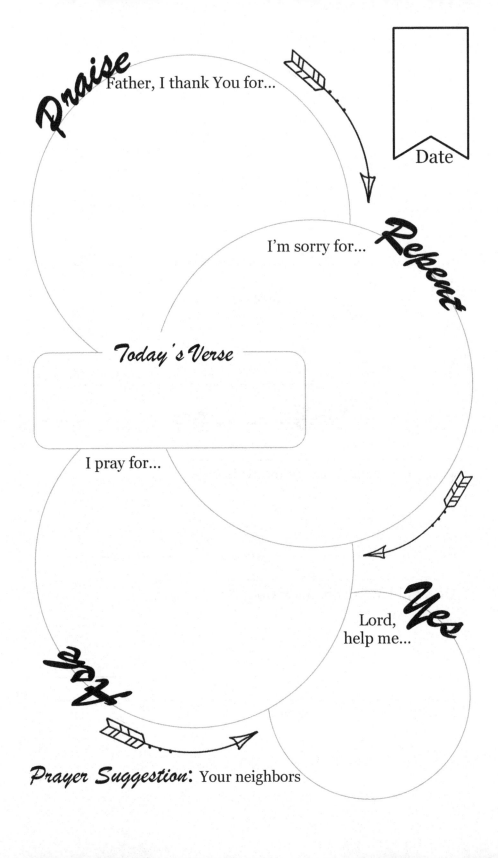

I am grateful for... *Gratitude*

Jesus, I hear You say... *Abide*

In Christ, I am... *Declare*

What am I celebrating in my life?

How did I see the hand of God?

In what ways was I a giver?

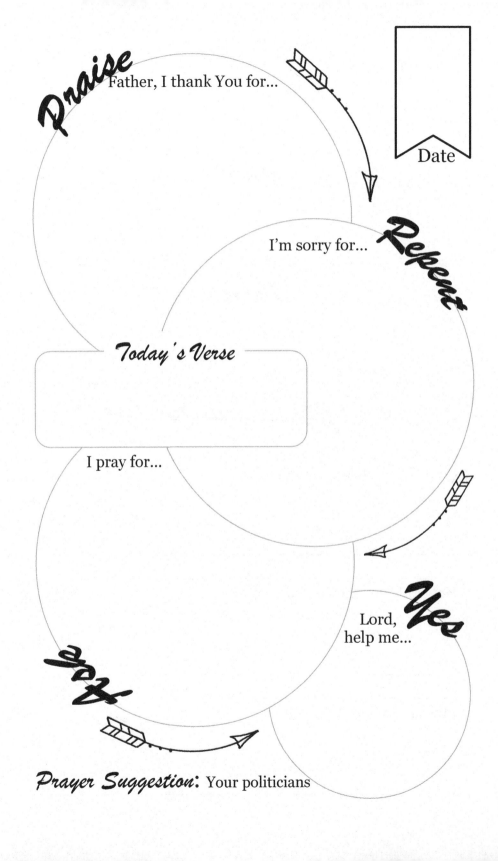

Gratitude

I am grateful for...

Abide

Jesus, I hear You say...

Declare

In Christ, I am...

What success did I have today?

How did I see the hand of God?

In what ways was I a giver?

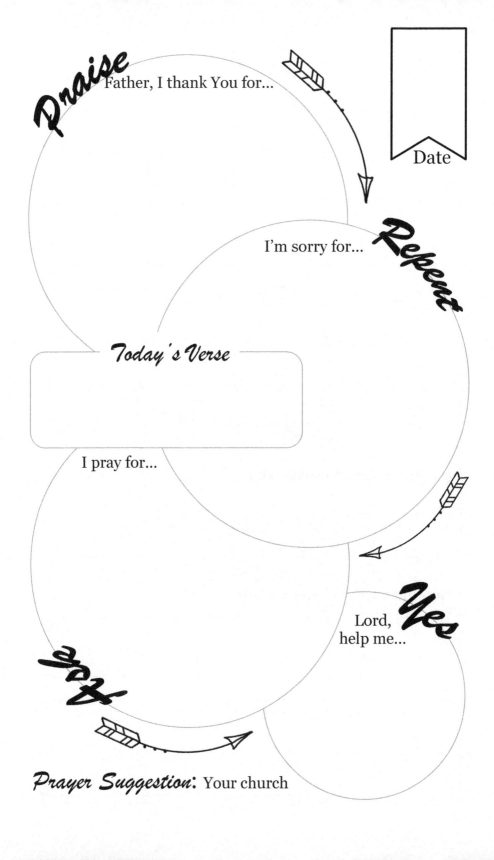

Gratitude

I am grateful for...

Abide

Jesus, I hear You say...

Declare

In Christ, I am...

What am I happy about in my life?

How did I see the hand of God?

In what ways was I a giver?

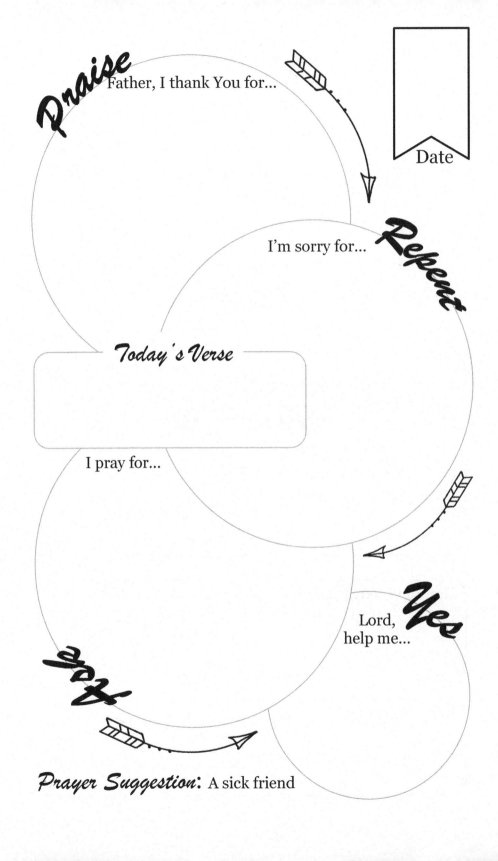

Gratitude
I am grateful for...

Abide
Jesus, I hear You say...

Declare
In Christ, I am...

What am I proud of in my life?

How did I see the hand of God?

In what ways was I a giver?

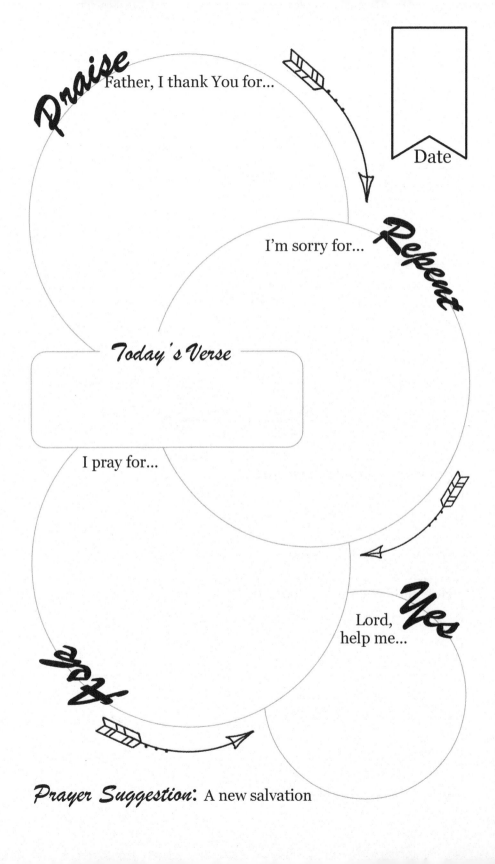

Gratitude
I am grateful for...

Abide
Jesus, I hear You say...

Declare
In Christ, I am...

What am I enjoying the most in my life?

How did I see the hand of God?

In what ways was I a giver?

Weekly Reflection

Prayers

Answered Prayers

Highs

What amazing things happened? How have these added to the quality of my life?

Thank God for goodness and blessing. Ask for His power and strength for next week.

Lows

What did I learned? What can I do differently?

Ask for forgiveness, if necessary, and for the grace to change.

Goal

What's one step I will take to move closer to my purpose?

Love Challenge

What's one act of service or random kindness I will do?

Notes

Notes

Notes

YOU CAN PRAY
for anything,
AND IF YOU
believe that
YOU'VE
received it,
IT WILL BE YOURS

Mark 11:24

Prayer Suggestions

You've finished your first week! Great work!

You can continue repeating the prayer suggestions from the previous week. Or you can switch it up and use some of the prayer suggestions below for daily prayer inspiration. Pick a prayer for the day and write it down in the space beside "Prayer Suggestion" at the bottom left corner of the page.

1. A Bible teacher
2. A business owner
3. A charity
4. A community service worker
5. A country at war
6. A decision you need to make
7. A foster child
8. A local community issue
9. A local elementary school
10. A local high school
11. A local hospital
12. A local university
13. A local women's shelter
14. A miracle you want to see god perform
15. A person on welfare
16. A person who serves you
17. A person with a disability
18. A refugee
19. A senior's home
20. A single father
21. A single mother
22. A social injustice
23. A teacher
24. A widow
25. A world religion
26. Addiction

27. An elderly person
28. An immigrant
29. An orphan
30. An unresolved conflict
31. Animal cruelty
32. Area of life needing victory
33. Attitude
34. Boldness to shine
35. Child poverty
36. Child slavery
37. Child soldiers
38. Choices
39. Country of choice
40. Current event in the news
41. Deliverance
42. Emotions
43. Entertainer/Actor
44. Environment
45. Faith
46. Fears
47. Finances
48. Foreign mission field
49. Forgiveness
50. Fruit of spirit your lacking
51. Gambling addictions
52. Gangs
53. Gender equality

54. Health
55. Homelessness
56. Human trafficking
57. Integrity
58. Juvenile youth
59. Kids church
60. Local mission group
61. Local politician
62. Mail carrier
63. Marriage
64. Mind
65. Missionary family
66. Obedience
67. Parenting/children
68. Past and future
69. Pastor
70. Person hard to love
71. Police
72. Pornography addictions
73. Priorities
74. Prisons
75. Prostitution
76. Protection
77. Purpose
78. Repentance
79. Reputation
80. Self image
81. Sexuality
82. Someone in the media
83. Something on mind/heart
84. Something that makes you angry
85. Something you feel guilty about
86. Something you lack peace in
87. Something you need

88. Spiritual gifts
89. Stranger you meet
90. Temptations
91. The justice system
92. Walk and talk
93. Wisdom
94. Work
95. World hunger
96. World peace
97. World sanitation
98. Young adults
99. Your country
100. Your dentist
101. Your doctor
102. Youth ministry

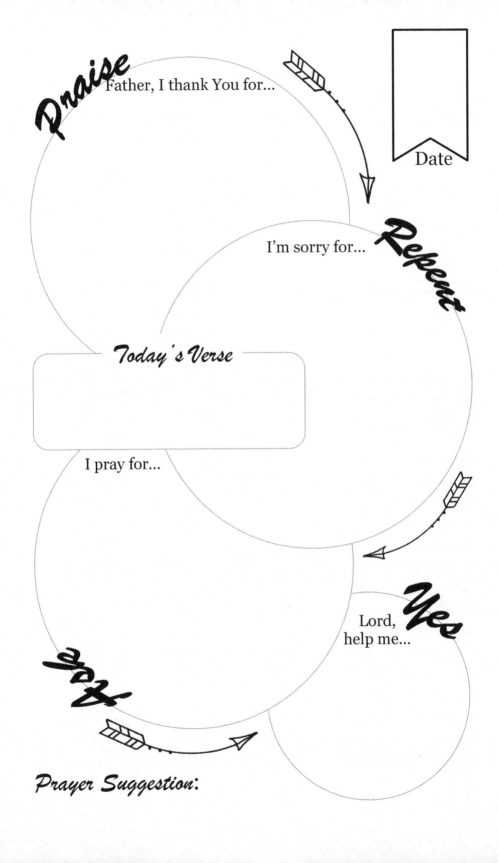

Gratitude

I am grateful for...

Abide

Jesus, I hear You say...

Declare

In Christ, I am...

What made me smile today?

How did I see the hand of God?

In what ways was I a giver?

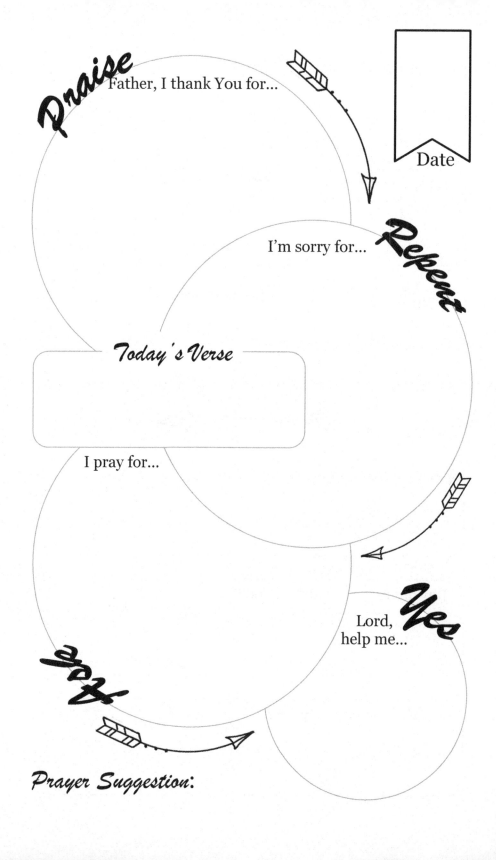

I am grateful for... *Gratitude*

Jesus, I hear You say... *Abide*

In Christ, I am... *Declare*

What am I excited about in my life?

How did I see the hand of God?

In what ways was I a giver?

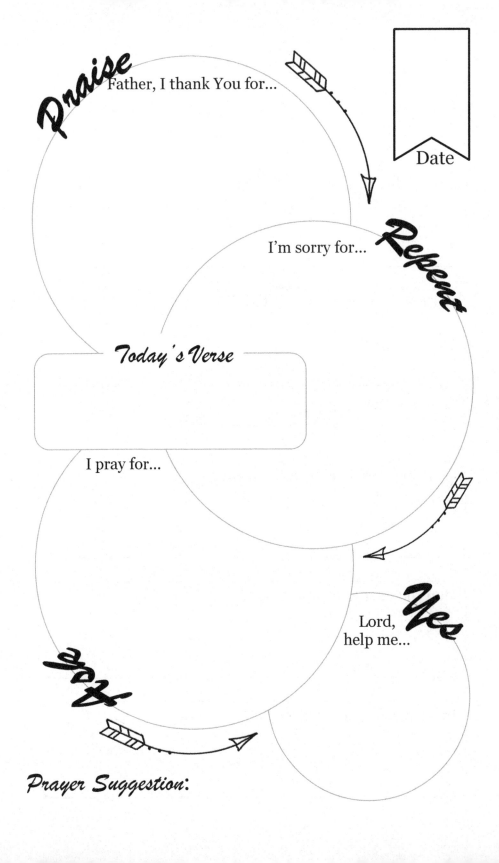

I am grateful for... *Gratitude*

Jesus, I hear You say... *Abide*

In Christ, I am... *Declare*

What am I celebrating in my life?

How did I see the hand of God?

In what ways was I a giver?

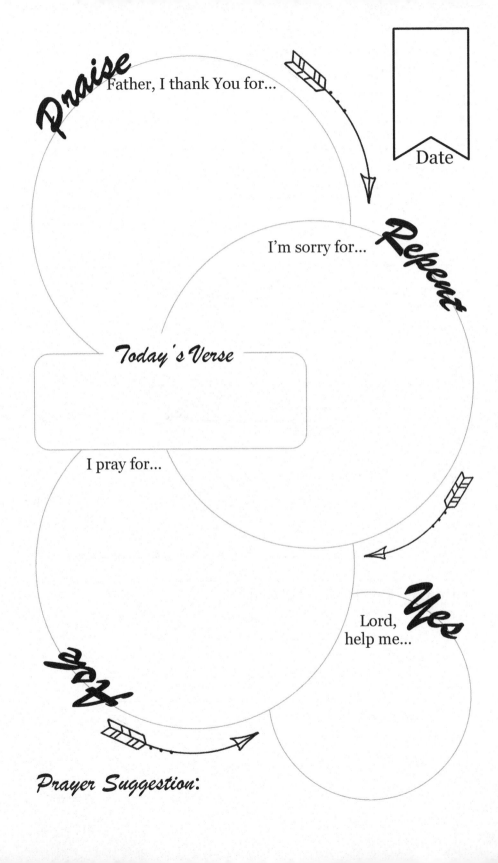

Gratitude
I am grateful for...

Abide
Jesus, I hear You say...

Declare
In Christ, I am...

What success did I have today?

How did I see the hand of God?

In what ways was I a giver?

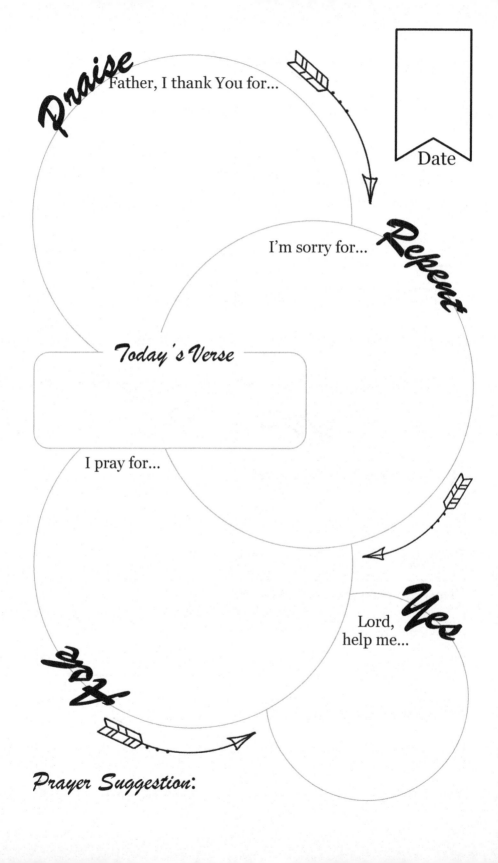

I am grateful for... *Gratitude*

Jesus, I hear You say... *Abide*

In Christ, I am... *Declare*

What am I happy about in my life?

How did I see the hand of God?

In what ways was I a giver?

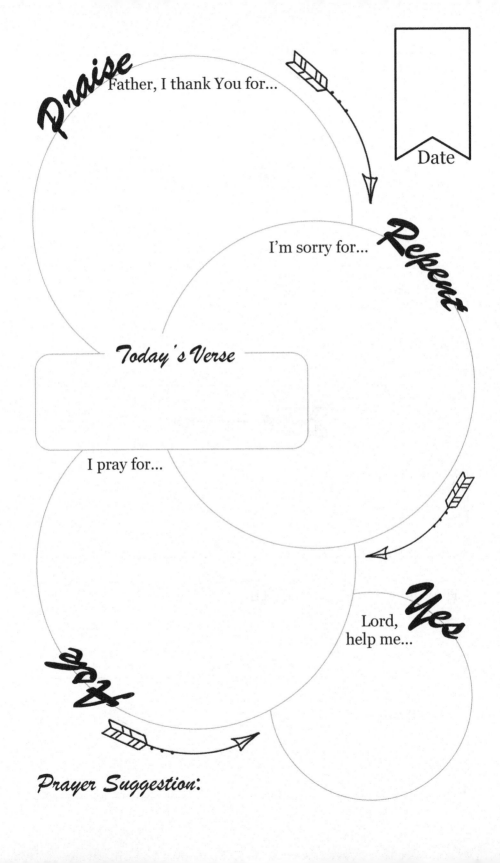

Gratitude

I am grateful for...

Abide

Jesus, I hear You say...

Declare

In Christ, I am...

What am I proud of in my life?

How did I see the hand of God?

In what ways was I a giver?

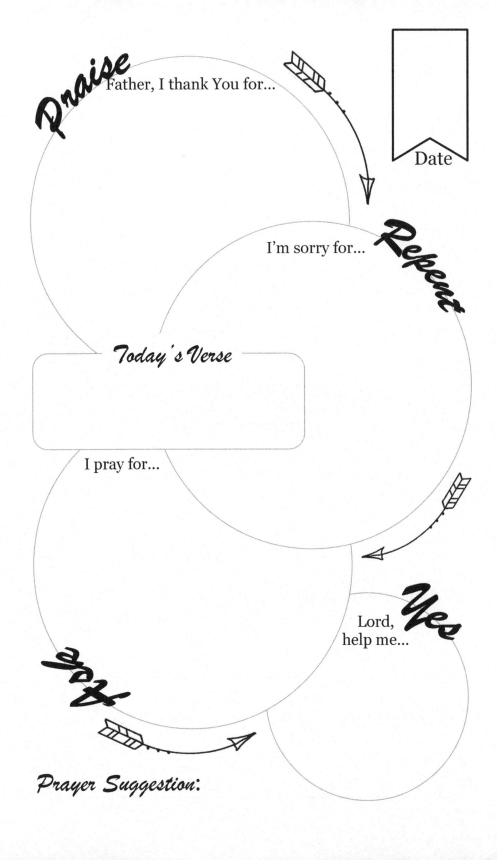

Gratitude

I am grateful for...

Abide

Jesus, I hear You say...

Declare

In Christ, I am...

What am I enjoying the most in my life?

How did I see the hand of God?

In what ways was I a giver?

Weekly Reflection

Prayers

Answered Prayers

Highs

What amazing things happened? How have these added to the quality of my life?

Thank God for goodness and blessing. Ask for His power and strength for next week.

Lows

What did I learned? What can I do differently?

Ask for forgiveness, if necessary, and for the grace to change.

Goal

What's one step I will take to move closer to my purpose?

Love Challenge

What's one act of service or random kindness I will do?

Notes

Notes

Notes

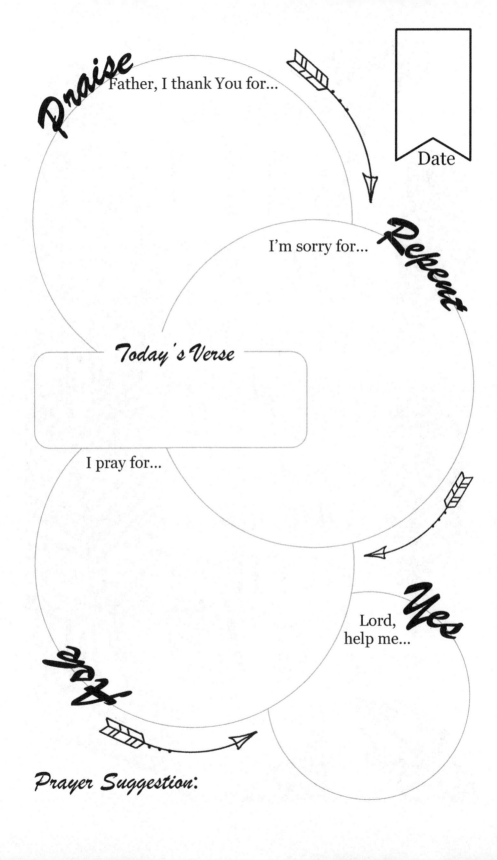

I am grateful for... *Gratitude*

Jesus, I hear You say... *Abide*

In Christ, I am... *Declare*

What made me smile today?

How did I see the hand of God?

In what ways was I a giver?

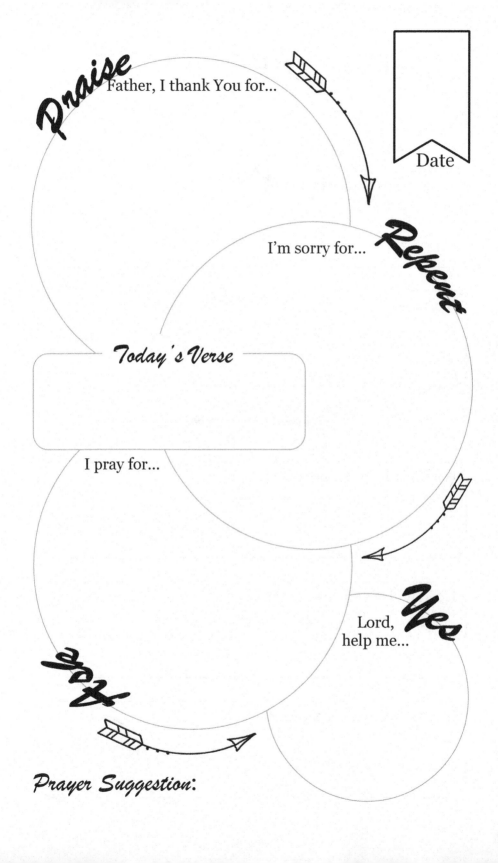

Gratitude

I am grateful for...

Abide

Jesus, I hear You say...

Declare

In Christ, I am...

What am I excited about in my life?

How did I see the hand of God?

In what ways was I a giver?

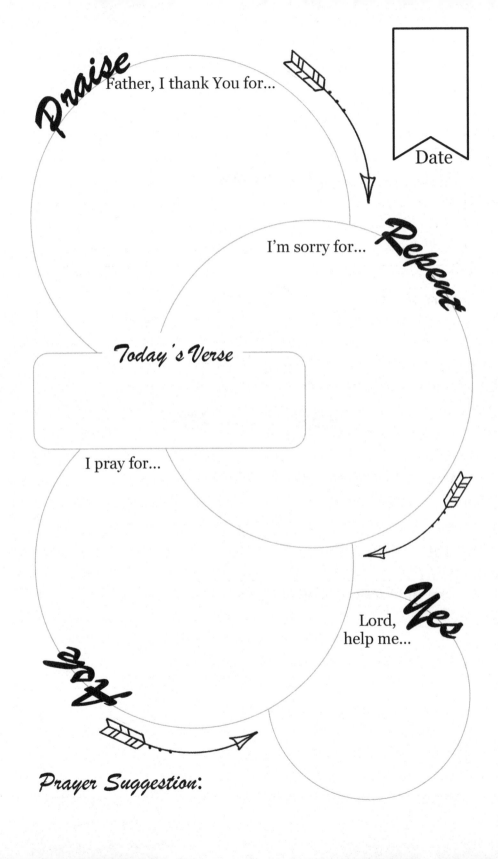

Gratitude
I am grateful for...

Abide
Jesus, I hear You say...

Declare
In Christ, I am...

What am I celebrating in my life?

How did I see the hand of God?

In what ways was I a giver?

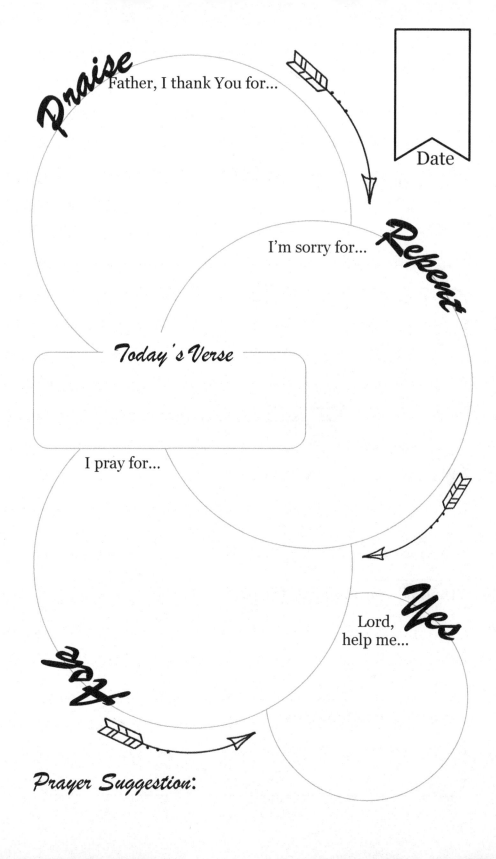

I am grateful for... *Gratitude*

Jesus, I hear You say... *Abide*

In Christ, I am... *Declare*

What success did I have today?

How did I see the hand of God?

In what ways was I a giver?

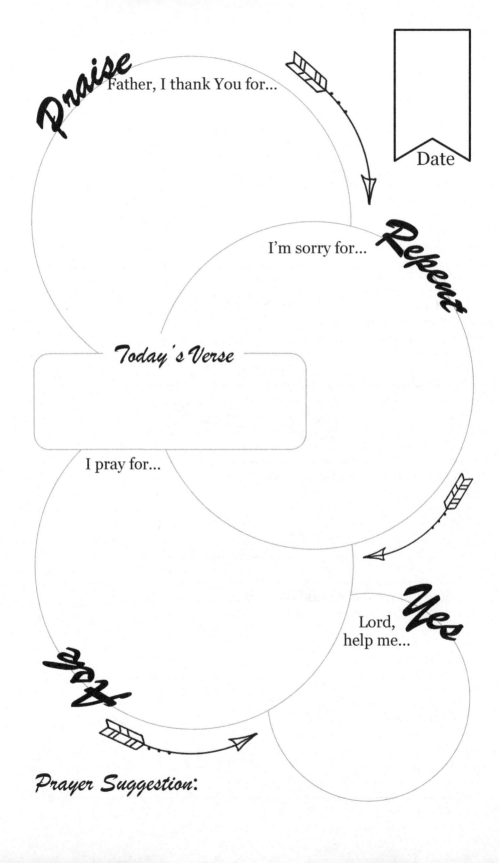

Gratitude

I am grateful for...

Abide

Jesus, I hear You say...

Declare

In Christ, I am...

What am I happy about in my life?

How did I see the hand of God?

In what ways was I a giver?

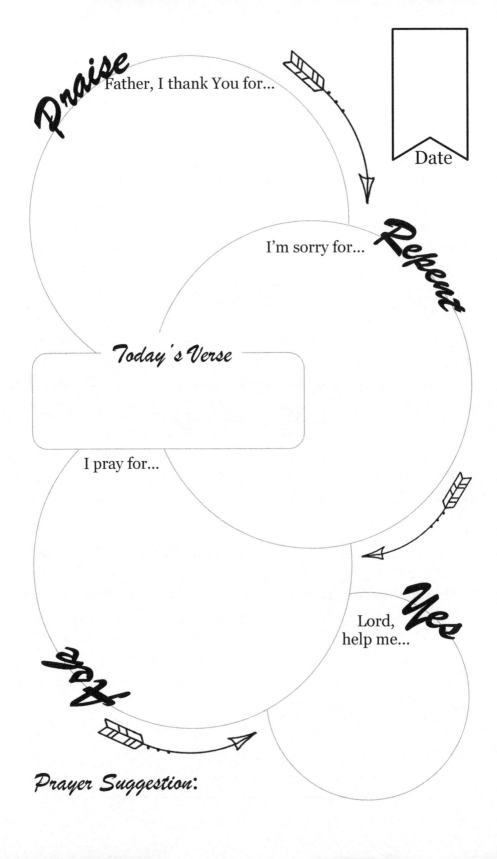

Gratitude

I am grateful for...

Abide

Jesus, I hear You say...

Declare

In Christ, I am...

What am I proud of in my life?

How did I see the hand of God?

In what ways was I a giver?

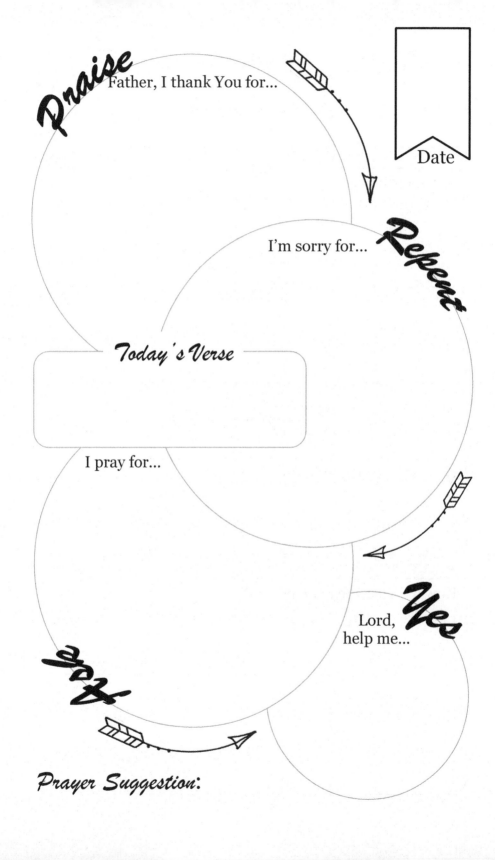

I am grateful for... *Gratitude*

Jesus, I hear You say... *Abide*

In Christ, I am... *Declare*

What am I enjoying the most in my life?

How did I see the hand of God?

In what ways was I a giver?

Weekly Reflection

Prayers

Answered Prayers

Highs

What amazing things happened? How have these added to the quality of my life?

Thank God for goodness and blessing. Ask for His power and strength for next week.

Lows

What did I learned? What can I do differently?

Ask for forgiveness, if necessary, and for the grace to change.

Goal

What's one step I will take to move closer to my purpose?

Love Challenge

What's one act of service or random kindness I will do?

Notes

Notes

Notes

COME TO ME,

ALL YOU WHO ARE WEARY **AND BURDENED,** AND I WILL GIVE YOU REST.

Matthew 11:28

Are you smiling yet?

Look how far you've come! Just one more week to go!

To ensure you don't miss a beat, order your next prayer journal so it can arrive after this one is complete.

Whether you've skipped some days, a couple weeks or months, keep going! God's not mad at you. He just wants to be close and hear your inner most thoughts and desires.

Visit Amazon to order your next copy

https://amzn.to/2OuBe9J

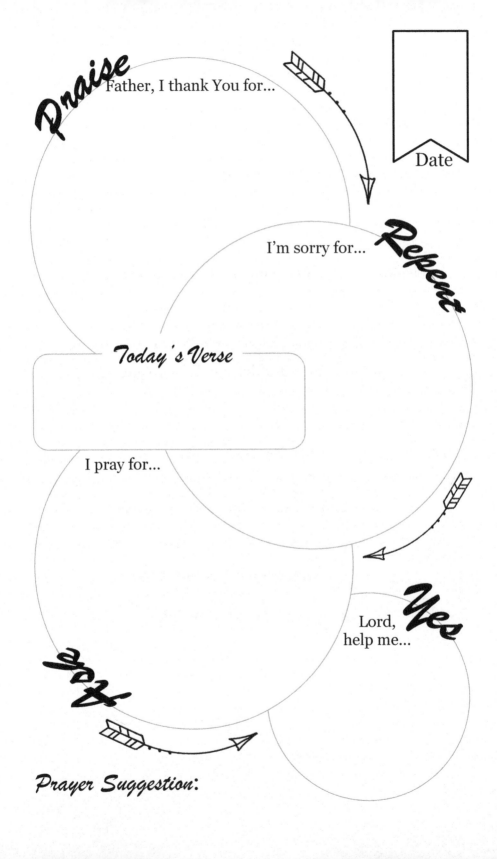

I am grateful for... *Gratitude*

Jesus, I hear You say... *Abide*

In Christ, I am... *Declare*

What made me smile today?

How did I see the hand of God?

In what ways was I a giver?

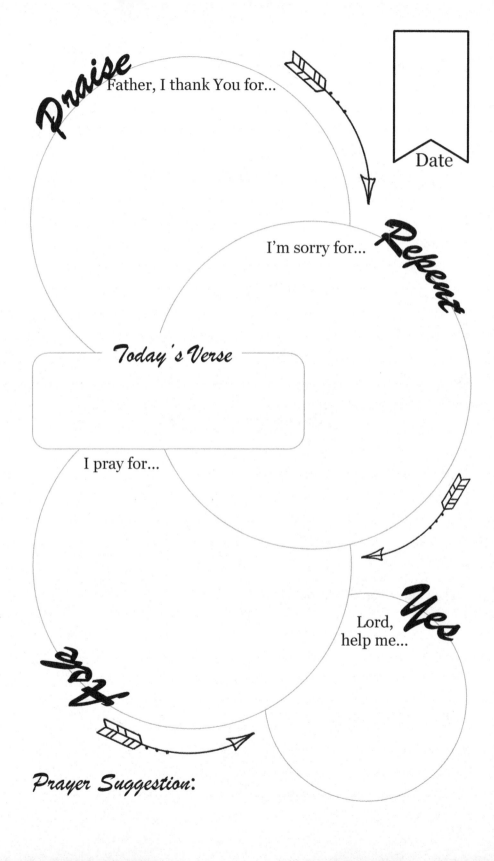

I am grateful for... *Gratitude*

Jesus, I hear You say... *Abide*

In Christ, I am... *Declare*

What am I excited about in my life?

How did I see the hand of God?

In what ways was I a giver?

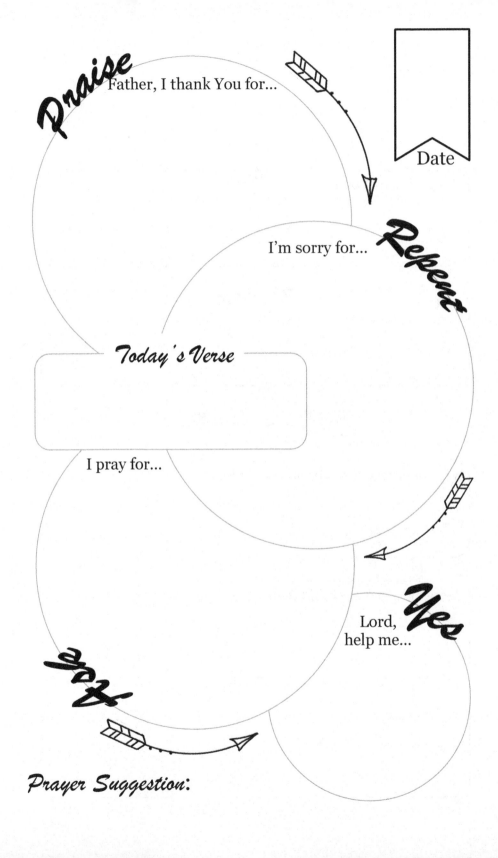

Gratitude
I am grateful for...

Abide
Jesus, I hear You say...

Declare
In Christ, I am...

What am I celebrating in my life?

How did I see the hand of God?

In what ways was I a giver?

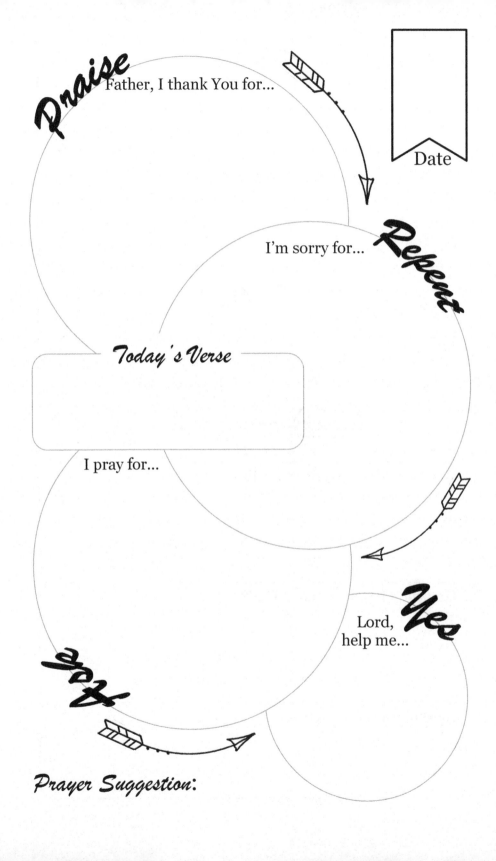

I am grateful for...   *Gratitude*

Jesus, I hear You say...   *Abide*

In Christ, I am...   *Declare*

What success did I have today?

How did I see the hand of God?

In what ways was I a giver?

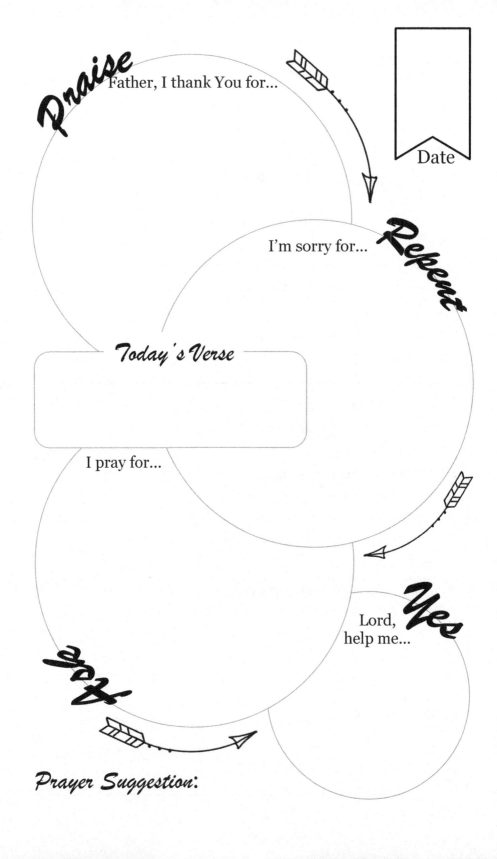

I am grateful for... *Gratitude*

Jesus, I hear You say... *Abide*

In Christ, I am... *Declare*

What am I happy about in my life?

How did I see the hand of God?

In what ways was I a giver?

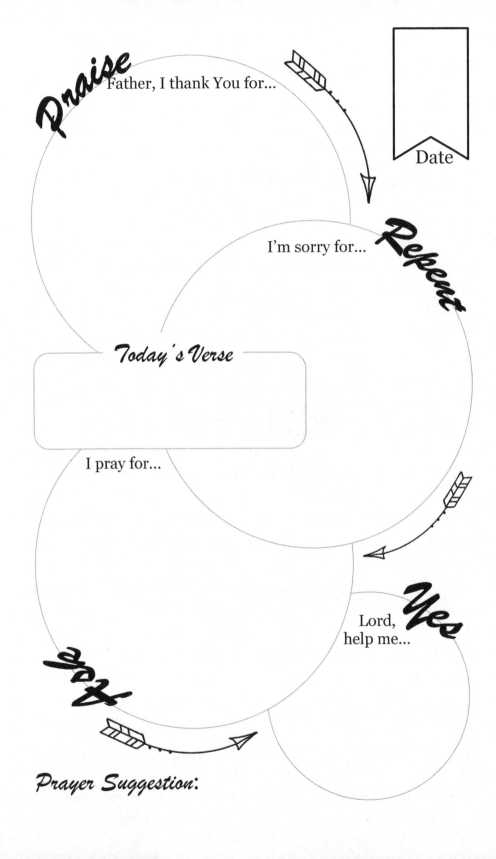

Gratitude

I am grateful for...

Abide

Jesus, I hear You say...

Declare

In Christ, I am...

What am I proud of in my life?

How did I see the hand of God?

In what ways was I a giver?

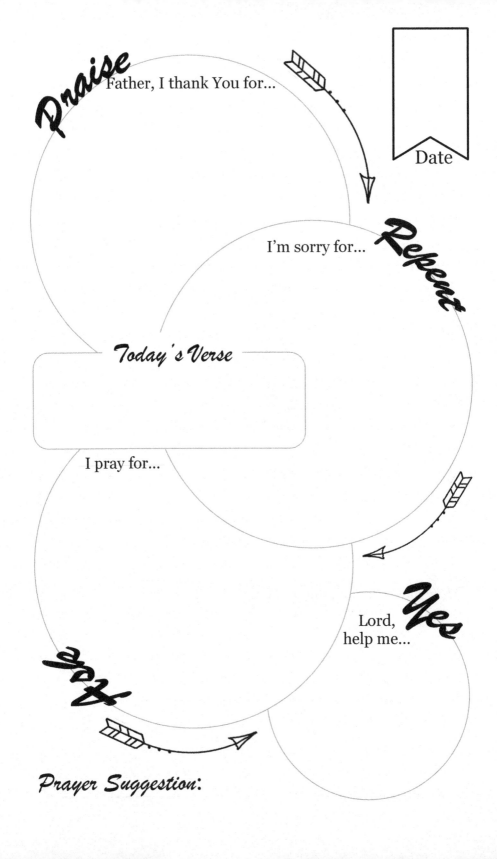

I am grateful for... *Gratitude*

Jesus, I hear You say... *Abide*

In Christ, I am... *Declare*

What am I enjoying the most in my life?

How did I see the hand of God?

In what ways was I a giver?

Weekly Reflection

Prayers

Answered Prayers

Highs

What amazing things happened? How have these added to the quality of my life?

Thank God for goodness and blessing. Ask for His power and strength for next week.

Lows

What did I learned? What can I do differently?

Ask for forgiveness, if necessary, and for the grace to change.

Goal

What's one step I will take to move closer to my purpose?

Love Challenge

What's one act of service or random kindness I will do?

Notes

Notes

Notes

You did it! Give yourself a high five!

Congratulations!

Whether you finished the journal in 1 month or 1 year, you persevered and stuck with it.

Celebrate!

Keep the momentum going and chase after God.

Because of your prayers, the world is a better place! Thank you for being diligent and giving the devil a kick in the teeth. You may never know the impact of your prayers on yourself, friends, family and the world until you reach Heaven.

> *"No matter how good things are, they can get better.*
> *No matter how bad they are, they can get better.*
> *So God only has one thing in His mind for*
> *your future and that's better." – Joyce Meyer*

I've often heard that it takes 21 days to form a habit. Contrary to that common belief, current research suggests it actually takes an average of 66 days to create a new habit. That means you're almost half way there! I encourage you to keep going in whatever shape or form is best suited for your life - whether it's with another prayer journal or in your own special way.

In the meantime...keep praying! And if you haven't already, order your next prayer journal so you can plunge even deeper into your relationship with Jesus!

> *"And it is impossible to please God without faith.*
> *Anyone who wants to come to him must believe that*
> *God exists and that he rewards those*
> *who sincerely seek him." – Hebrews 11:6*

You can find your new copy on Amazon: **https://amzn.to/2OuBe9J**

Final Thoughts

Thank you for purchasing my *first* book! I also want to thank you for trusting me to walk you through this journey. I am confident that you've come out on the other side bearing fruit in your relationship with Christ and in the world around you. I acknowledge you for making prayer a priority in your walk with God and for taking a stand for the loved ones in your life. You had a vision for how life could be and you took the necessary steps to get there.

Now it's time to be honest. Did this book make you smile?

I truly hope that you smiled...on numerous occasions! And if you did find yourself smiling, would you be willing to share with others? I've made a conscious choice to not be on social media, but I'm hoping that you are. I'm really depending on the support of my readers to share my book with their friends, family and the world around them.

A simple review on Amazon or a social media post is all it takes to make the world a better place. Imagine how many people would be actively praying on a daily basis, and how many more smiling faces you would see!

So keep on smiling because it makes others smile. And please connect and share your stories with me.

With gratitude and deep thanks,

Kristina
joypublishingkindle@gmail.com

Recommended Resources

I've read all three of these books and have bookmarked the prayers in each chapter. Then each day, I pick a prayer from each book to pray for the day.

The Power of a Praying Woman – Stormie Ormartian

https://amzn.to/2pCGWez

The Power of a Praying Parent – Stormie Ormartian

https://amzn.to/2BZvReX

The Power of a Praying Wife – Stormie Ormarian

https://amzn.to/2Pd3z4g

I've read this book twice. Once when I was a new Christian and again when my brother said he was interested in reading it. He was inspired by Michael Phelps who had read the book around 2016 when it saved him from suicide.

The Purpose Driven Life – Rick Warren

https://amzn.to/2BX22vA

Made in the USA
Coppell, TX
30 April 2020